Twelve Days of Christmas

12 Advent Readings

A.J. Wolfe

ISBN: 978-1-7311-0354-3

The only book that should ever be written is one that flows up from the heart, forced out by the inward pressure. When such a work has gestated within a man it is almost certain that it will be written. The man who is thus charged with a message will not be turned back by any blasé consideration. His book will be to him not only imperative, it will be inevitable. –*The Pursuit of Man, The Divine Conquest of the Human Heart*, A.W. Tozer

To my Granny,
Merry Christmas.

Forward: The Longing and the Voice

I am in constant awe of the Bible. You can read the same verses and stories repeatedly, and then one day something hits you. You see something you didn't see before; you understand something about Jesus that you never understood before. This miracle experience is defined as a "revelation," and it is common to all believers. The Bible describes itself this way, *"For the word of God is living and active, sharper than any two-edged sword, piercing to the division of soul and of spirit, of joints and of marrow, and discerning the thoughts and intentions of the heart," (Hebrews 4:12).* The book- The Bible is *"living and active"*... How can a book be alive and active?

The answer is found in the next verse. *"And no creature is hidden from his sight, but all are naked and exposed to the eyes of him to whom we must give account," (Hebrews 4:13).* The Bible is alive and active because God is alive and active! *"No creature is hidden from HIS sight."*

The Bible says, *"Holy, holy, holy is the Lord of hosts; the whole earth is full of his glory!"(Isaiah 6:3).* The earth is full of his glory means that we are able to clearly see how real God is by looking at the things God has made. In his letter to the Romans, the apostle Paul says, *"For what can be known about God is plain to them, because God has shown it to them. For his invisible attributes, namely, his eternal power and divine nature, have been clearly perceived, ever since the creation of the world, in the things that have been made. So they are without excuse," (Romans 1:19-20).* God didn't stop speaking when he spoke creation into existence; he is actively speaking truths into the world through his Holy Spirit. Some examples of this are the changing of seasons, the birth of babies, sunrise, sunsets and so much more.

The birth of Jesus is typically focused on during the Christmas season. I wholeheartedly believe we should read it often. It is the most incredible story of how God was longing for us. It is filled with God's tender emotions, his determination to give us Jesus, and the overwhelming joy that he gets to communicate with us now. The angel told Joseph, *"Behold, the virgin shall conceive and bear a son, and they shall call his name Immanuel (which means, God with us)." (Matthew 1:23).* When you love someone, you want to be with them. God wasn't shaking his head in frustration, mad that he had to send Jesus to the earth. His longing to be near us was so great, he sent his only son. He made plans to be with us. God wants to look at us, embrace us, and have conversation with us. The origin of the word Christmas is "Christs" "Mass."[1] "Christ" referring to Jesus and "mass" referring to the tradition of taking communion. Taking communion symbolizes being joined to Christ Jesus in his death and resurrection, which enabled us to freely communicate with God, without a priest or animal sacrifice. *"But God, being rich in mercy, because of the great love with which he loved us, even when we were dead in our trespasses, made us alive together with Christ-by grace you have been saved-and raised us up with him and seated us in heavenly places in Christ Jesus,"(Ephesians 2:4-6)*. God sent Jesus to live sinless, die as our eternal sacrifice, and be resurrected so that we can personally commune with God. Communion then is not a monologue but a dialogue; it is two people exchanging their thoughts and feelings[2]. Prayer is just that: spending time and communicating with God.

The goal of this devotional is to show people how big and grand, powerful, and majestic God is, yet he gently draws us to himself. This God, who spoke creation into existence and parted the Red Sea, whispers to us wisdom and knowledge as he did to the first disciples, *"I give thanks to my God always for you because of the grace of God that was given you in Christ Jesus, that in every way you were enriched in him in all speech and knowledge-" (1 Corinthians 1:4-5).* He predestines and coordinates situations in our lives to reveal to us that He is real and He is good. He longs greatly to reveal to people who he really is: happy and joyful. God says that we are his joy. *"You make known to me the path of life; in your presence there is fullness of joy; at your right hand are pleasures forevermore, (Psalm 16:11).* In his "presence" means being with Him. God giving us joy is not separate from God being with us. He doesn't drop the gift off on the porch, get back in the car, and drive away. He is the joy! We experience the gift of his love for us when we are spending time with Him in His presence.

      We can experience God and his goodness. Our eyes can be opened to his hand in our life, and our ears can be opened to hear the voice of the only true God. As you read about the arrival of Jesus on earth, my prayer for you is that your heart will open up, and light will come pouring in. I pray you will steal away to pray, *"Lord open my eyes to see you, open my ears to hear you"*. This life for whom Jesus chooses to reveal himself to is a glorious life; it is a full life, abundant with God's surprises. *"Ask, and it will be given to you; seek, and you will find; knock, and it will be opened to you. For everyone who asks receives, and the one who seeks finds, and to the one who knocks it will be opened," (Matthew 7:7-8).*

1.
December 13th

"And as Moses lifted up the serpent in the wilderness, so must the Son of Man be lifted up, that whoever believes in him may have eternal life," (John 3:14-15).

John 3:1-21

It may seem unusual to start a Christmas devotional with the death of Jesus rather than his birth, but his death and resurrection were the reason for his arrival. In the preceding passage of scripture, Jesus is speaking with Nicodemus. Nicodemus was a Pharisee, which meant that he was a religious man and was a ruler of the Jews. Nicodemus came to Jesus in the night and said, *"Rabbi, we know that you are a teacher of God, for no one can do the things you do unless God is with him," (John 3:2)*. Nicodemus was referring to the miracles that Jesus had been performing in the community. Jesus responded to Nicodemus, *"Truly, truly I say unto you unless one is born again he cannot see the kingdom of God," (John 3:3).* Nicodemus was an educated teacher of the law, yet he could not understand what Jesus meant. Nicodemus was trying to figure out how a person can go back in the womb after they have already been born. Jesus was talking about a spiritual birth, not a physical one, *"Do not marvel that I said to you, 'You must be born again. The wind blows where it wishes, and you hear its sound, but you do not know where it comes from or where it goes. So it is with everyone who is born of the Spirit," (John 3:7-8).* Jesus then proceeds to reference a story about the Israelite people in the sacred scriptures. The people of Israel were enslaved to King Pharaoh in Egypt for four hundred years. Through a series of plagues Pharaoh let the people go. As they were leaving, Pharaoh changed his mind and sent his army after them. The Israelites were upon the Red Sea and had no escape route. God parted the waters of the sea so the people got through and then caused the water to trap and kill the Egyptians when they followed suit. Moses led the people into the wilderness, where they began to become impatient about their future and unthankful for their current provisions… *"And the people became impatient on the way. And the people spoke against God and against Moses, "Why have you brought us up out of Egypt to die in the wilderness? For there is no food and no water, and we loathe this worthless food," (Numbers 21:4-5).* God sent fiery serpents among the people to bite them. The people asked Moses to pray to God to take the serpents away. *"And the Lord said to Moses, "Make a fiery serpent and set it on a pole, and everyone who is bitten, when he sees it, shall live," (Numbers 21:8).* Moses made a serpent out of bronze, and, if anyone who was bitten looked up at it, they would live rather than die from the snake bite. This event in the desert foreshadowed the death of Jesus on a cross. The serpent bite represents a death that cannot be escaped but by looking up to the Cross. Looking is believing, [3] and seeking equals finding[4]. Speaking to Nicodemus, Jesus was recalling a past event, but also foretelling the future of his death and the spiritual rebirth he was going to make available by it. This is the purpose of the Season of Advent. It is a reflection on events past and a turning of the gaze forward to what lies ahead. Jesus was born through a physical birth as a baby so we could be born again into a spiritual birth.

> "For to us a child is born, to us a son is given; and the government shall be upon his shoulder, and his

name shall be called Wonderful Counselor, Mighty God, Everlasting Father, Prince of Peace. Of the increase of his government and of peace there will be no end, on the throne of David and over his kingdom, to establish it and to uphold it with justice and with righteousness from this time forth and forevermore. The zeal of the Lord of hosts will do this," (Isaiah 9:6-7).

2
December 14th

"Therefore the Lord himself will give you a sign. Behold, the virgin shall conceive and bear a son, and shall call his name Immanuel," (Isaiah 7:14).

Matthew 1:18-23

Mary and Joseph were engaged to be married. Getting pregnant outside of marriage was dangerous for a woman in Mary's era; she could be stoned to death if public officials found out. The implications for Joseph's reputation were severe as well. Joseph and Mary were likely in an arranged marriage situation, but it is possible that they were very much in love. Mary conceiving a child by supernatural means caused fear for each of them and required a lot of faith to even believe it. Joseph was a just man, and unwilling to make a public spectacle out of Mary, resolved to break their agreement to be married quietly. Joseph may have been heartbroken that his betrothed was taken by another man. An angel of the Lord appeared to Joseph in a dream and encouraged him to move forward with Mary. The angel addressed Joseph by name, *"Joseph, son of David, do not fear to take Mary as your wife, for that which is conceived in her is from the Holy Spirit. She will bear a son, and you shall call his name Jesus, for he will save his people from their sins," (Matthew 1:20-21).* Can you imagine Joseph's emotions after being visited by an angel, being told his fiancé had not been unfaithful to him, to marry her, that they were going to have a son, the name of their son, and that the miracle son is the Savior?! Imagine the weight of the news Joseph had just received; his questions must have been many. Yet, trying to sort through all he had heard, similarly to us; he landed in the sweet hammock of those words, *"...they shall call his name Emmanuel which means, God with us."* Joseph and Mary had heard and believed the words of the prophet Isaiah read in the synagogue. They were anticipating this Savior with the rest of the Jewish community. They never would have imagined they would in fact be the parents of this Savior! The name of Jesus[5] in Hebrew means "Rescuer", "Deliverer". The same God who was with Mary and Joseph is the God who is with us reading these words.

God reveals himself to us through the same Holy Spirit that put Jesus in the womb of Mary.

"For God so loved the world, that he gave his only Son, that whoever believes in him should not perish but have eternal life. For God did not send his Son into the world to condemn the world, but in order that the world might be saved through him," (John 3:16-17).

3.

December 15th

"The voice of the Lord makes the deer give birth and strips the forest bare, and in his temple all cry, "Glory!" (Psalm 29:9)

Luke 1:1-11

Zechariah and Elizabeth "were righteous before God, walking blamelessly in all the commandments and statutes of the Lord," (Luke 1:6). They had no children and were past childbearing age. Zechariah was a priest who was chosen this particular year to "Enter the temple of the Lord and burn the incense. And the whole multitude of the people were praying outside at

the hour of incense," (Luke 1:9-10).
According to the custom of priesthood, he would only be picked one time in his life to burn incense in the Most Holy Place of the temple. Zechariah and Elizabeth must have waited in much anticipation for that day when Zechariah was able to enter into the place where there is no barrier between God and man. "There I will meet with thee, and I will commune with thee from above the mercy seat, from between the two cherubims which are upon the ark of the testimony, of all things which I give thee in commandment unto the children of Israel," (Ex 25:22, KJV). During the hour of incense, Zechariah would take coals only from the brazen alter (the place

where animal sacrifices were made to God for the sins of the people), and two handfuls of sweet incense. After this, he would walk through the Holy Place, and beyond the veil, into the Holy of Holies where he would "put the incense on the fire before the Lord, that the cloud of incense may cover the mercy seat that is over the testimony, so that he does not die," (Lev 16:13).

Zechariah's hands may have trembled as he lit the incense on the mercy seat. After all, he could die if he had sin in his life or if he came in direct contact with the power and person of God. God arranged the events of Zechariah's life to speak to him at this exact moment, "And there appeared to him an angel of the

Lord standing on the right side of the altar of incense," (Luke 1:11). The hour of incense represents the melding of prayers from Gods people and the eventual blood sacrifice of Jesus that was going to make a way for us to have complete access to the throne of God through prayer alone. Animal sacrifices were no longer going to be needed, not just for the saints of old but for you and me today. The good news of the gospel is that unencumbered access to God is available to us forever. Our sins that so easily weigh us down are eradicated in the blood sacrifice of Jesus who is our high priest forever. Now, like the Psalmist, we can freely offer up that sweet incense in our hour of prayer. "Let my prayer be counted as incense before you, and the lifting up of my hands as the evening sacrifice," (Psalm 141:2).

"Since then we have a great high priest who has passed through the heavens, Jesus, the Son of God, let us hold fast our confession. For we do not have a high priest who is unable to sympathize with our weaknesses, but one who in every respect has been tempted as we are, yet without sin. Let us then with confidence draw near to the throne of grace, that we may receive mercy and find grace to help in time of need,"(Hebrews 4:14-16).

4.
December 16th

"Therefore he is the mediator of a new covenant, so that those who are called may receive the promised eternal inheritance, since a death has occurred that redeems them from the transgressions committed under the first covenant," (Hebrews 9:15).

Luke 1:11-24

Here is the one time Zechariah is chosen to burn the incense at the hour of incense-the place where God communes with man, and an angel appears! All the people are outside praying along with him. I wonder if Zechariah really believed that God was going to speak to him in some way. Maybe he had already talked to the other priests and some had mentioned how burning the incense was not what they expected. Little did Zechariah know, an angel was going to show up! Have you ever noticed in the Bible how, if a person comes in contact with an angel, they are immediately afraid? The angel says, *"Do not be afraid, Zechariah, for your prayer has been heard, and your wife Elizabeth will bear you a son and you shall call his name John,"* (Luke 1:13). I love that the angel calls him by name. Put your name where Zechariah's is, "Do not be afraid_____." Zechariah and his wife Elizabeth were past childbearing years, and from this angel's message, we can tell that Zechariah had been praying about it, *"...for your prayer has been heard..."* (v.13). Zechariahs responded to the angel's message in a seemingly normal way according to the text, *"How can this be?"(v.18),* I can picture myself asking the same question. I can imagine praying about the same thing for so long that I don't really believe that prayer is going to be answered. And the message wasn't just, you are going to have a son, but you are going to have a son who is going to be great to the kingdom of God! Zechariah is a priest who dedicated his life to scripture and prayer and belief in God. The angel is telling Zechariah what is to be, and moreover, that a miracle is going to take place. This son of Zechariah and Elizabeth, who is known as John the Baptist, has been predestined to come into the world to go before Jesus, *"He will turn many of the children of Israel to the Lord their God...to make ready for the lord a people prepared,"(Luke 1:16, 17).*

Baby John was going to prepare the way of another miracle baby: Jesus. The final and everlasting covenant between God and man would come through this baby Jesus.

"Now faith is the assurance of things hoped for, the conviction of things not seen. For by it the people of old received their commendation," (Hebrews 11:1).

5.
December 17th

"Behold, I am the servant of the Lord; let it be to me according to your word," (Luke 1:38).

Luke 1:26-38

Growing up Jewish Mary read and studied the Hebrew Scriptures. The Jewish people were waiting on the Messiah that they read and wondered about. Mary must have been in amazement that God chose her to bear and mother the Son of God! God is making a new and everlasting covenant with all of humanity through a young Jewish woman. *"And behold, you will conceive in your womb and bear a son, and you shall call his name Jesus. He will be great and will be called the Son of the Most High. And the Lord God will give to him the throne of his father David, and he will reign over the house of Jacob forever, and of his kingdom there will be no end," (Luke 1:31-33).* Mary's initial response to the angel is much like Zechariah's, *"How will this be since I am a virgin?"*(v. 34) *The* angel assures Mary that the Holy Spirit will do the work, and nothing is impossible with God. Mary responds to the angel's message with an announcement about who she is. Notice Mary's word choice of *"Behold,"* which essentially means pay attention to what I am about to say. *"Behold, I am the servant of the Lord..." (v.37).* Mary may have had a revelation that she is loved for who she is and not for what she can do, *"Greetings O favored one, the Lord is with you!...Do not be afraid, Mary for you have found favor with God,"(v.28, 30)*. Mary knew who she was: a servant of the Lord. A servant[4] is defined as a person in service of another[4]. She defined her life as in service to God. She knew who she was because of the grace that had been given her prior to finding out about being the mother of Jesus. This is a marked experience that some of us have yet to experience as well. We are loved by God because of the grace that has been given to us despite what we do or have done. May our immediate heart response to God's plans be like Mary's, *"Let it be to me according to your word," (Luke 1:38)*.

> "Only fear the Lord and serve him faithfully with all your heart. For consider what great things he has done for you," (1 Samuel 12:24).

6.
December 18th

"Thus the Lord has done for me in the days when he looked on me, to take away my reproach among people," (Luke 1:25).

Luke 1:39-45

The angel told Mary that her old aunt Elizabeth was going to have a baby boy! Mary left quickly to visit Aunt Elizabeth and her belly confirmed the angel's message. We hear Elizabeth's outlook on her miracle pregnancy by her words, *"to take away my reproach among people," (Luke 1:25)*. Elizabeth was referring to the shame that was associated with not being able to conceive a child. She was, after all, married to Zechariah, who was serving as priest before God. In the Old Testament, barrenness of the womb was considered an absence of God's presence. Elizabeth must have believed this to be the case for most of her life, since we know she did not conceive until she and Zechariah were advanced in years. "Reproach"[5] is defined as: to find fault with or blame. Shame was woven throughout the days of Elizabeth's life. She felt an absence of God, who predestined her biblical commendation as one who was *"righteous before God, walking blamelessly in all the commandments and statutes of the Lord," (Luke 1:6).* Do you ever feel shame about something? Maybe you have gone through a really tough season of life and don't feel the presence of God or have never felt God near to you. The good news is that one of the names of Jesus is Emmanuel, God with us. Elizabeth may have felt like something was wrong with her the majority of her life because she couldn't conceive a child. Little did Elizabeth know, she was going to carry the cousin of Emmanuel! The children of God are promised that God will never leave them. God says, *"I will never leave you nor forsake you," (Hebrews 13:5)*. If you are going through a season of life where you do not feel the nearness of God, it is a promise that he is with you as he was with Elizabeth all of those years. God does not break his promises, and he does not lie. We may not get all of the things we want or understand the ways of God, but we can choose to trust that he knows exactly what he is doing. He is a good Father who coordinated all of the events and circumstances of the people in the Bible to bring us Jesus. As we look back on these events, let us remember God's faithfulness to us.

"He found him in a desert land, and in the howling waste of the wilderness; he encircled him, he cared for him, he kept him as the apple of his eye. Like an eagle that stirs up its nest, that flutters over its young, spreading out its wings, catching them, bearing them on its pinions, the Lord alone guided him, no foreign god was with him," (Deuteronomy 32:10-12)

7.
December 19th

Mary's Song of Praise: The Magnificat

"…And blessed is she who believed that there would be a fulfillment of what was spoken to her from the Lord," (Luke 1:45).

Luke 1:45-56

Heavenly knowledge was being revealed in the town of Judah. Mary and Elizabeth were experiencing revelations of God's greatness in the confirmation of each other's pregnancies. When Mary entered her aunt's home and greeted her, Elizabeth's baby jumped in her womb. Elizabeth, immediately humbled by the presence of Jesus mother asked, *"And why is this granted to me that the mother of my Lord should come to me?"(Luke 1:43)*. At the sound of Mary's voice, Elizabeth knew that what was spoken by the angel was true and commended Mary's faith. *"And blessed is she who believed that there would be a fulfillment of what was spoken to her from the Lord," (Luke 1:45)*. Can you envision Mary and Elizabeth embracing each other, in wonderment at the plans of God? These women had faith! They are heroes of our faith. They didn't doubt the angel's news; they didn't respond with fear or worry. The correspondence between their humility and their faith is to be noted. We see Elizabeth's humility when she asked, *"Why is this granted to me…?"(Luke 1:43)*. We see Mary's humility when she states, *"Behold, I am the servant of the Lord...,"* (*Luke 1:38).* Mary traveled to Judah from Nazareth because she believed that Elizabeth, who was barren as long as Mary knew her, was now pregnant. I imagine Mary recounted the angel's words on her way to Elizabeth's house, *"Nothing will be impossible with God," (Luke 1:37).* Mary's conversation with Elizabeth quickly turns to a song of praise as she is overcome with the realization of how great God is and how small she is in comparison. Mary's song is known as "The Magnificat,[7]" which in Latin means, "My soul magnifies the Lord". Her praise was in response to God's promise before she received the promise. A song of faith rose up in Mary because *"she believed there would be a fulfillment of what was spoken to her from the Lord," (Luke 1:45). Let* us ponder the blessed virgin's faith and may her faith spur us on to believe the promises of the Lord for ourselves.

"And Mary said, "My soul magnifies the Lord, and my spirit rejoices in God my Savior, for he has looked on the humble estate of his servant. For behold, from now on all generations will call me blessed; for he who is mighty has done great things for me, and holy is his name" (Luke 1:46-47).

8.
December 20th

"In those days John the Baptist came preaching in the wilderness of Judea, "Repent, for the kingdom of heaven is at hand," (Matthew 3:1-2).

Luke 1:57-80

It must have been difficult for Elizabeth to have a mute husband during her miracle pregnancy. I can imagine the questions they both had bubbled to the surface daily. Faith presided in the face of fear. The angel that appeared to Zechariah in the temple said their baby would be *"great before the Lord, he will be filled with the Holy Spirit, to go before him, to make ready for the Lord a people prepared," (See Luke 1:15-17)*. When the time came for baby John to be circumcised, Zechariah was still mute. Tradition would dictate that the first born son would be named after his father, yet Elizabeth said, *"No, he shall be called John," (Luke 1:60).* Zechariah wrote on a tablet, *"His name is John," (Luke 1:63).* In that moment God gave Zachariah the ability to speak again, and he was filled with the Holy Spirit and began to prophecy about his son John's life purpose. *"And you, child will be called the prophet of the Most High; for you will go before the Lord to prepare his ways...," (Luke 1:76).* John was purposed by God to go before the ministry of Jesus and to prepare the hearts of the people. The Israelites were God's chosen people but not because of anything extraordinary that they had or did. He chose them solely because he loved them (See Deuteronomy 7: 7-8). God wanted to reveal his son Jesus to the Jews and Gentiles alike. John the Baptist prepared the hearts of the people in the local community with the message, "Repent and be baptized". To "repent[8]" means you feel sorry for your previous actions or behavior and you have the conscious thought to pursue a change of heart and mind. Baptism is a symbol of your recognition of this new change caused by God's grace. *"To give knowledge of salvation to his people in the forgiveness of their sins, because of the tender mercy of our God," (Luke 1:77-78).* It is in

God's character to have mercy. John baptized with water as a symbol of man's response to God's pursuit of the human heart. Jesus baptizes us with the Holy Spirit, who continually leads us into truth and is the seal of our salvation[9].

"I have baptized you with water, but he will baptize you with the Holy Spirit," (Mark 1:8).

9.
December 21st

"Fear not, for behold, I bring you good news of great joy that will be for all the people. For unto you is born this day in the city of David a Savior, who is Christ the Lord," (Luke 2:10-11).

Luke 2:1-21

Joseph and Mary traveled to the city of Bethlehem to register for a census. While they were there, Mary was going into labor. They searched for a room to rent for the birth, but there was not a room available anywhere. These events lead them to a stable where Mary gave birth to Jesus, the Savior of the world. Mary *"wrapped him in swaddling clothes and laid him in a manger,"* (v.7). The parents of Jesus must have had many questions for their God. As they were in the stable and Mary is surely exhausted from birth, they see men coming towards them. Joseph on his guard may have been looking for a piece of wood lying around, ready to defend his wife and newborn son. The men turned out to be sent from God. These guys were shepherds who were on the midnight shift watching their flock. They were out in a field nearby when an angel appeared to them, *"Fear not, for behold, I bring you good news of great joy that will be for all the people. For unto you is born this day in the city of David a Savior, who is Christ the Lord. And this will be a sign for you: you will find a baby wrapped in swaddling cloths and lying in a manger," (Luke*

2:10-12). Right after the angel gave this message, a large group of heavenly beings lit up the night sky. It must have been sublime! *"And suddenly there was with the angel a multitude of the heavenly host praising God and saying, "Glory to God in the highest, and on earth, peace goodwill toward men," (Luke 2:14 KJV)*. It was as if heaven couldn't contain them; the angels had to slip through the atmosphere to rejoice at their Savior's birth on earth. The Bible says that the shepherds got up quickly to go find the baby. They came looking for a baby, but they were an encouragement to Mary and Joseph as well. The shepherds shared what the angel had spoken to Mary and Joseph, confirming once again who their first born son was. We see God coordinating these events and details.

He brought shepherds out of nowhere in the middle of the night to witness the birth of the Savior. He gives signs and performs miracles still to this day. He uses people, places and things to reveal his glory, his peace and his goodwill towards mankind.

"I am the good shepherd. I know my own and my own know me, just as the Father knows me and I know the Father; and I lay down my life for the sheep. And I have other sheep that are not of this fold. I must bring them also and they will listen to my voice. So there will be one flock, one shepherd," (John 10: 14-16).

10.
December 22

" 'And you, O Bethlehem, in the land of Judah, are by no means least among the rulers of Judah; for from you shall come a ruler who will shepherd my people Israel,' "(Matthew 2:6).

Matthew 2:1-12

After the birth of Jesus, a group of wise men were following a star from the East to Jerusalem and were inquiring about the location of the king of the Jews. The reputation of these wise men likely preceded them as renowned astronomers. Their admittance of seeing this newborn's star in the east and following it was shocking to King Herod. This intelligent group of men came following this star, in order to worship this newly born King! Herod, deeply troubled by their inquiry, gathered together the chief priests and scribes and asked them where this Christ was to be born. They told him, *"...in Bethlehem of Judea," (Luke 2:5).* King Herod told the wise men to let him know when they found the baby Christ, so that he could come and worship him too. After the wise men left King Herod, the star that lead them there, rose back into the sky. They followed it until it rested over the house that the child Jesus was in and *"they rejoiced exceedingly with great joy," (v.10).* The wise men went in, and when they saw Jesus with his mother, *"they fell down and worshipped him. Then, opening their treasures, they offered him gifts, gold and frankincense and myrrh," (Matthew*

2:11). These wise men came to worship this King that was prophesied about in the scriptures. An angel came to the wise men and warned them not to return back to King Herod. King Herod and the Jewish people were spiritually blind to what kind of King that Jesus was. Herod ordered a massacre of all the boys two years and under in an effort to kill the baby Jesus. As Jesus grew and began teaching and doing miracles, the people could not discern Jesus words, his actions, or even who he was. Jesus is King of Kings; there is no end to his kingdom. No one is going to overtake his throne, because his throne is a spiritual one. His reign goes on forever and ever. The prophets of old prophesied of a coming King, the wise men brought gifts and worshiped the newborn

King. When Jesus was crucified, the sign over him read, 'King of the Jews'. When Jesus was resurrected from the dead, he ascended back to Heaven to sit on the throne, at the right hand of his Father God. Do you hear the voice of the King?

Pilate: "Are you the king of the Jews?"

Jesus: "Do you say this of your own accord, or did others say it to you about me?"

Pilate: "Am I a Jew? Your own nation and chief priests have delivered you over to me. What have you done?"

Jesus: "My kingdom is not of this world. If my kingdom were of this world, my servants would have been fighting, that I might not be delivered over to the Jews. But my kingdom is not from the world."

Pilate: "So are you a king?"

Jesus: "You say that I am a king. For this purpose I was born and for this purpose I have come into the world-to bear witness to the truth. Everyone who is of the truth listens to my voice," (John 18:33-37).

11.
December 23

"May the God of hope fill you with all joy and peace in believing, so that by the power of the Holy Spirit you may abound in hope," (Romans 15:13).

Luke 2:22-32

Why did Simeon and Anna spend their life in the temple? They were old, and they had been longing for God for a long time. Simeon was, *"...waiting for the consolation of Israel," (v.25).* Anna was, *"waiting for the redemption of Jerusalem," (v.38)* If you have been longing for something, there must be a period of time in which you have been waiting for it. Simeon, being guided by the Holy Spirit, went to the temple. When he saw baby Jesus, he took him in his arms. Simeon was taking in his little eyes and his little nose, and he began to worship God. Simeon was worshiping God for fulfilling his longing. God kept his promise to Simeon that *"he would not see death before he had seen the Lord's Christ," (Luke 2:26).* Today, Jesus is taking people into his arms just as Simeon did and worshiping God because of his great love for his children. A father and mother rejoice simply that their child is theirs. Our Father in Heaven rejoices over us! The revelation of Jesus Christ is that God loves you. There is no barrier between you and him that he has not broken down through Jesus. *"But God shows his love for us in that while we were yet sinners, Christ died for us," (Romans 5:8).* There is absolutely nothing that can keep God's love from you; it's not even your choice. It is too powerful, it is bigger than you, and it is stronger than even death. *For I am sure that neither death nor life, nor angels nor rulers, nor things present nor things to come, nor powers, nor height nor depth, nor anything else in all creation, will be able to separate us from the love of God in Christ Jesus our Lord," (Romans 8:38-39).* God created within us a longing to be satisfied. Contentment is a rarity in this world we live in. People always seem to disappoint us. Places in life become dull. Material things are never enough. Money will keep you chasing it. Take heart dear reader. What you are longing for is a person and his glory will satisfy you. "*For*

God, who said, "Let light shine out of darkness," has shone in our hearts to give the light of the knowledge of the glory of God in the face of Jesus Christ,"(2 Corinthians 4:6). The truth is not a denomination, a religion or a mysterious code to be cracked. The truth is a person whose name is Jesus. He is a Father, a brother, and a friend. His love is so strong that death could not even keep him in the grave. He is alive, and he has joined us to God. "See *what kind of love the Father has given to us, that we should be called children of God, and so we are," (1 John 3:1).*

"Set your hope fully on the grace that will be brought to you at the revelation of Jesus Christ," (1 Peter 1:13).

12.
December 24th

"For Jews demand signs and Greeks seek wisdom, but we preach Christ crucified, a stumbling block to Jews and folly to Gentiles, but to those who are called, both Jews and Greeks, Christ the power of God and the wisdom of God,"(1 Corinthians 1:22-24).

Luke 2:33-40

A baby dedication is a joyous occasion where friends and family are invited to come to a place of worship and join in welcoming a new little child into the spiritual covenant of God's people. Mary and Joseph were greeted by Simeon upon their arrival at the temple. They were standing right beside him as Simeon took their eight day old baby and gave blessing to God. Within that worshipful moment, Simeon declared that this baby is "*...a light for revelation to the Gentiles, and for glory to your people Israel,*" *(Luke 2:32)*. Simeon finished blessing God, turned to Mary specifically, and prophesied the death of her son. This doesn't seem very joyous for a baby dedication. Mary's thoughts may have sounded something like this, *"but the angel said that he would be the son of the most high, that his throne would never end, that he would reign forever, that he is holy! Those shepherds came out of nowhere to proclaim that this boy is the Christ, a savior! What about the wise men who followed a star to our home and bowed down and worshiped our son saying he was king of the Jews?!*" The baby Jesus was being dedicated at the temple to

God as a symbol that he would live the life that God planned for him. God planned that he should die and be resurrected. Mary would be heartbroken, of course, that she should witness the murder of her son on a cross by the request of their own people. Jesus was born Holy, and though he was tempted with all sin as we are, he did not sin. When Jesus was crucified, he was a perfect sacrifice, and he tore down the curtain that kept us out of the Holy of Holies. Only the high priest could go into that most holy place to commune with God, but now we can too. An animal sacrifice and a priest are no longer necessary to talk to God, Jesus, and the Holy Spirit. The holiness God requires, in order to stand in front of him and have a conversation with him, we now possess through the blood sacrifice and resurrection of Jesus. This is the true beauty of the Christmas story; this is the good news of great joy! *"But now in Christ Jesus you who once were far off have been brought near by the blood of Christ. For he himself is our peace," (Ephesians 2:13-14).* Mary and Joseph were simple people, and God chose them to show the world how much he loves the people that he made. God is not in stained glass windows. He is not so far away that he cannot see and hear you. God chose these people and these events because he desired so greatly to have you know his love and his care for you. As we look back on the birth of Jesus, we can't help but look forward with joyful expectation. This is the hope of the gospel, *"The mystery hidden for ages and generations but now revealed to his saints. To them God chose to make known how great among the Gentiles are the riches of the glory of this mystery, which is Christ in you, the hope of glory," (Colossians 1:26-27).*

"Because, if you confess with your mouth that Jesus is Lord and believe in your heart that God raised him from the dead, you will be saved," (Romans 10:9).

Notes

Unless otherwise indicated, Scripture quotations are from: The Holy Bible, *English Standard Version.* © 2001 by Crossway, a publishing ministry of Good News Publishers. All rights reserved.

1. Dictionary.com. (n.d.). Retrieved from http://www.dictionary.com
2. Dictionary.com. (n.d.). Retrieved from http://www.dictionary.com
3. Tozer, A.W. (2009). *The pursuit of God: The human thirst for the divine. Milton Keynes: Authentic Media.*
4. Matthew 7: 7-8
5. Jesus (name). (2018, October 23). Retrieved

from http://www.wikipedia.org/
6. Dictionary.com. (n.d.). Retrieved from http://www.dictionary.com
7. Dictionary.com. (n.d.). Retrieved from http://www.dictionary.com
8. Dictionary.com. (n.d.). Retrieved from http://www.dictionary.com
9. John 16:13, Ephesians 1:13

Made in the USA
Middletown, DE
11 December 2018